False Indigo

sheeba arifeen

[False Indigo]: An outdoor flower that is almost never bothered by pests or disease

Dear Reader, the following is a story told through a collection of poems, slowly revealing two struggling souls, plagued with darkness. They meet each other, share lessons and insecurities, fall in and out of love. Betrayal, happiness, success, anxiety, empowerment -These poems use themes and emotions we've all experienced to explore life above all else content

life before boy meets girl

WINTER MOON

he finds himself

staring at the winter
moon

at 5 pm

wondering why

his insides are
darker

than the sky outside

LUCKY

she died in her arms

but

she still picks up
the phone sometimes

to call her

so many nights have
come and gone

but

she still sees her in
her dreams

and it's a nightmare
when

she wakes up

if she gave her
everything

why does she feel
like nothing?

TRANSLUCENT

it would be a long
way down a deep
dark hole

if you took the sun
and rolled it inside
his soul

a one-way ticket

down a two lane
road

he packed a bag,
doesn't plan to come
back

older, but not all
grown

wait, the shell of
the body

he's floating around

is his very own

TSUNAMI

she was an expert at
it

carrying the burden
of anxiety
instead of carrying
the conversation.

analyzing thoughts
before they formed,
criticizing them
once they were said

holding her breath
instead of her head

she wished her
words were
uninterrupted waves,

so her sentences
could flow

but too often, the
tides rolled and
crashed against

the sand and the
rocks,

pounding

the shore; her chest

if only she knew the
power of her force...

tsunami approaching

LABYRINTH OF LOVE

walking around with
broken hearts and
band aids

healing and waiting
to be healed.

growing up,

he was taught

loving oneself is
selfish

and loving someone
else is foolish

so he produced all
this love and it had
nowhere to go

stored it on the
shelf, poured it in a
bail, but maybe no
one knows

serotonin turns sour

if you let love sit
still too long, it
becomes angst

and he rages and
wonders why love is
so difficult

it's because we've

trapped ourselves

expelled ourselves

robbed ourselves

forgotten how it
feels

THIRTY HOURS

it was only when she
spent the night
awake
in a hospital room
with no windows
staring across at the
bed

when

she realized she was
only about as
supportive as the
chair she was sitting
in

she wished there was
something she could
do

but

she had no clue.

for someone who
writes so much,

most of the time,
she is at a loss for
words

UNFRIENDED

as she sat across
from him speaking,

he couldn't hear her
words

there was the
screeching sound of

the death of a
friendship

bells he overlooked,
ringing like warning
signs

guess he didn't show
up to book club
they were no longer
on the same page

he began to wonder

how to bury a
relationship

that was already six
feet under

there is no eulogy

"I would kindly
never like to see
you again."

IF YOU LIKE FRUIT

put her in your
basket

take her home

peel her

for she is a fruit

vibrant, all-natural

ask the hard
questions

as she opens up,

let her sweet sugar
drip

fill your insides
with the saccharine
aroma

do not let her rot;

do not bruise or
neglect her.

pick her,

but only if you like
fruit

cue trouble

INNOCUOUS
BEHAVIOUR

we're all familiar
with that game
pretend to forget her
first name

but he knew her last
one too

dancing like a fool
all night

thinking he fooled
her alright
celebrate and chalk
up a win

but he went fishing
in a lake

she wasn't even
swimming in

after a few glances
and dances,

evaluated his
chances

they're looking good

she's looking good

but at the end of the
night,

she looked him in
the eyes

softly apologized,
caught him by
surprise

and said,

"I didn't catch your
name or I must've
forgot."

wide-eyed, with a
smirk on the side,

"Please forgive me."

she served it boldly

SING-A-LONG

some people

are songs you don't
understand the first
time you hear them

but one day,

you catch yourself
humming

and it finally clicks

SWIMMING IN THE DEEP END

the signs were big

she knew she was
trespassing

the restricted
swimming pool.

to his surprise,

she jumped in with
an absence of
hesitation

the water was cold
like his
temperament,

critical he may be of
her swimming
abilities,

the deep-end is
unchartered territory

truthfully,

it was within her
knowledge

that her preference
and capabilities are
more appropriately

matched for the
shallows

still, together

they swam to great
depths

until

they reached waves
so strong,

coming up for air
became impossible

becoming acquainted

SHROUDED IN MYSTERY

she was the
brightest mystery
in the darkness that
became my life

she left no
guarantees
but I never felt more
safe
collateral-free

she never ceased to
amaze me,

made everything
look so easy

binge watching, I
was hooked

she was a real good
limited series show

and even if you
asked me
to search high and
low

i could not find the
words

to describe her

HEXED

he didn't come with
strings

but I was attached

his eyes

hooked me in

and how daunting
it's been

watching him walk
away

rather than towards
me

he didn't believe in
magic

but he casted spells

and I can surely tell

i am not the only
victim

pointless to wonder

how he did it

even more so to ask,

because everyone
knows,

a magician never
reveals their secret

CARPETS & RUGS

some of us are born
with a blanket that
grows with us. It is
the prop in the show
of our lives.

anything they didn't
like, I covered with
my blanket

and no matter what,

they told me;
never lift the
blanket

off your fears, your
weaknesses, your
vulnerabilities

so I left it laying
there

but the blanket that
kept me safe and
warm,
it became a rug

i swept everything
under,
with quivering faith,
hoping or wondering

if anyone will ever
lift up and see all
that I've hidden

ENCHANTE

tell me all the dumb
things

you did in your
childhood

that resulted in
those scars on your
body

tell me about the
bruises I can't see

tell me what you did
every New Years'
Eve

let me meet the you
that made you, you.

take me to that spot
in the city that was
your escape

tell me how you
spent your worst
birthday

and about the times
you didn't think it'd
ever be okay

I want to know every
place you've seen

and everything
you've been

through

let me meet the you

before I met you

MIRACULOUS

introvert,

but sometimes a
little extra-vert

find me in the
corner

writing notes I'll
never read

to my future self

cheques to my
parents

still not enough to
fulfill my debts

don't spend a penny
on me but let me
give you the world

that is when I am
happiest

what kind of a
philosophy?

how I came to be

is still a mystery

the docs told her,
get rid of me

eleven months, no
recovery

but they saw a
vision

before they saw me

a marvel or a
miracle

the work of divine
agency

MUM

do you dare trifle
with the women

who allowed you her
space for nine
months?

how is it that,

the first day of your
life,

you've already met
the best person you
will ever know?

FRUGAL NOT FANCY

grew up, with not so
much, never
thinking we needed
more

a two-bedroom
apartment

dancing around a
wooden bunk bed in
hand-me-downs

with flyers scattered
around the floor
groceries were not a
chore,

we'd sit and circle
food of our liking

cutting out coupons,

not knowing we
would grow up to be
experts at
identifying steals,

the waiting period
of a good deal.

perfectly content
with never knowing
the inside of a
restaurant

so many home
cooked meals I'd
still choose over
eating out

perhaps our light-up
shoes were brighter
than those dimwits

who'd parade around
fancy, with our
names like
accessories hanging
from their mouths

barely knew what a
vacation meant
how could we care

where everyone
went?

all we were excited
for were trips to the
park, hanging from
monkey bars,
marking the spots in
the sand where we
jumped from the
swings

that was the closest
we got to flying

BABA

he tucked his dreams
away

into the back pocket
of his tattered jeans
hanging in the
corner of his closet

without him, I could
not have gotten here

his own education,
he traded in for a 20
year retail career

made a believer out
of me

taught me how to
live this life,
then built his own
around me

showed me survival
in this world,
then put me in the
center of his

he is the best man
I have ever known

EAT TOGETHER

it wasn't until later
on that I thought
about the impact of
sharing a meal;

look at the last
doughnut,

that goes uneaten
for days
because we all give
it up for one another

look at the five
rooms we leave
empty

all gravitating
towards the one with
the most noise,
just to fill it with
more

look at the face of
my mother
listening to our
stories, offering
advice

look at the
confidence of my
father
motivating us,
joking like a friend

you cannot get rid
of

look at the fabric

that is the
foundation

of this family,

tightly knit

slowly but with
great strength

people watching & sharing
lessons

HOW WEIRD

we are all victims of
no's and what if's.

at one point, the
intensity in our
presence and
brightness in our
eyes were
incomparable.
that was before all
this stress became
unbearable
why do the best
people end up with
fate so terrible?

is it odd we're all
an acquired taste?

how strange is life
and all its irony,

we settle on 'it's
meant to be'

in Old English,
weird used to mean
destiny

PROFILING

people, I believe are
more complex and
difficult to
comprehend than
their actions suggest

naive judgments
cloud our curiosity.

when we start
labeling people as
monsters,
we sacrifice our own
obligation to ask
how they became
that way

CAN I BUY A VOWEL?

maybe humans are

simply just
consonants

composed of a dozen
random letters,
strung together

walking around
without a clue

and we can't
pronounce ourselves

but we take shots at
all the other words

perhaps, we don't
contain any vowels

is this the reason
people are so hard
to read?

INTERNET MODELS

maybe we should all
lose our phones
so we can find
ourselves

talk real slow
to get our attention
spans back

dead end chats like
a cul-de-sac

waiting for the next
system upgrade

refreshing new
screens for old
updates

all present but not
together

likes are a unit of
measure

self-worth, self-
esteem
reputations to
redeem

we're all just over
thinkers, over-
lovers, overflowing

no one really cares
how it's going
when they ask
"how's it going?"

we all hate
ourselves but have
so much love to give

PLEASE NOTE:

people are not
garbage

but if you treat them
like they are,

they can easily make
a home

out of a trash can

SEASONS

days may end

and times may
change but the smell
each season brings
will always stay the
same

how remarkable it is

that simply the
weather can
transport us back in
time

involuntarily

CALLING LIBERTY

some people make
noise,

others stay silent

some people wave
flags,

others choose
violence

i didn't know then
but now it's making
more sense

there are people in
the middle east.

their hearts are full
but they don't eat

lies and bribes

people paying with
their lives

there is no weapon
quite as destructive
as

Power

FREEDOM

it felt for a second

like everything

was about to change

then they took them
away

to someplace so
strange

close enough they'll
say

while still out of
range

their dreams put on
hold

but the media's
entertained

no one ever came
into this world

asking to be
detained

CARDS

we are only as free
as they tell us we
are allowed to be

they deal the cards
in their hands

hold ours too

pre disposed to the
doom

all it takes is a
single

snap, clap and boom

to become a victim
of their addiction

they will tell you
what to say

and what to do and
what to wear

then they'll tell you
to proceed with care

don't you dare

believe you are free

SILENT LOVERS

sometimes, people
leave compliments
inside their own
heads

they admire people's
eyes, their jawline,
their voice, their
style

passively.

perhaps thinking
that their beauty is
so evident, so
obvious, they just

already know. they
must know.

silly lovers we are,

admiring humans
without
acknowledging them

UNCLAIMED ART

even those that
disagree

must admit to some
degree:

humans are art

everyone just wants
to meet someone
who looks at them as
if they were taking a
picture with their
eyes

struggling to
capture the
overwhelming view
composed of you

you all want to meet
someone who thinks
you are not quite
like anyone else
they've ever met
before

and it is in this
pursuit, more often
than not, that we
surrender and settle

through thick & thin

FREE ADVICE

if you are torn,

learn how to sew

MISSING MUDITA

it is not any less
great
if they do not
applaud you

it is not any less
wonderful
if they are not
happy

it is still a big deal
even if they make
you feel small

you should still
celebrate even if
they don't come to
your party

music is no less
different
if you're dancing
alone

you still deserve it

they know you
deserve it too

WHITE NOISE

leave the
background noise on
while you work
quietly

for noise has a
tendency to die
down

but if, conceivably
it does not,

do not get lost or
weary of its
vibrations

keep shining

light travels faster
than sound

MOTIVATED

the feeling that
someone
underestimates your
abilities

gets a special kind
of adrenaline
flowing through
your body

perhaps, there is no
force of motivation

quite like that of
someone telling you
can't do something

MORE FREE ADVICE

if one day you see

someone finds

your confidence

and your success

offensive,

keep offending the
offended

FAN CLUB

multiple people in
your crowd,

will wish failure
upon your plans

but they look like
fans.

most of the criticism

you will hear,

comes from the
people behind you

but the people
behind you are not
standing there to
catch you

just because their
view is your back,
doesn't mean they
got it

SHOVEL ALONE

people like to see
snow on your
driveway

they want to see you
struggle while you
shovel

they'll never tell
you that

hell, they might
even offer to help
you

but the second the
sun comes out and
melts away your
snow,

they wonder why
clouds still hang
above their driveway

they'll go home
bitter,

salty enough to melt
the snow away
themselves

RESULTS SPEAK

if you put heart into
your work,
someday it will be
worth it

you can plant a seed
and think no one
will see it
but once it grows
into a garden of
flowers,

people notice

people will stop and
smell them

INSIDE

you have to step out

of the box

to see the box

you've trapped
yourself in

or else,

you will only see
four walls and

mistake the box for
a room

but notice: there is
no door

maybe that is why,

opportunity never
knocks

inside your little
box

breaking barriers

BREAK A MIRROR,
BAD LUCK. MIRROR
BREAKS YOU, WORST
LUCK

I find it so strange
that a stranger can
point out our body's
natural obscurities
and then the
strangest things
become our
insecurities

I never thought
twice before raising
my hand

now, every thought I
have is filtered
down
before it reaches my
mouth
words are heavier
when we are little,
they let us grow up
feeling small
they shape us,
convince us
even when we're
smarter, we carry
them with us

why am I ashamed -
like the bags on my
face
aren't the nights
that I spent
working hard to get
to this place

like the colour of
my skin
and the ordinary
brown of my eyes
don't hold the fight
of my ancestral
tribes,
and signify the dirt
that soaked up the
blood of their lives

I never thought
about brows
or the hair on my
arm
until someone
pointed it out
why did I think they
were right about,
my face and my body

everything about me
was fine
until someone told
me
to fix what is mine

RETROGRADE

when you feel
empty,

remember that even
the moon

does not stay full

PETTY CASH

if you could convert
confidence into
currency,

all you would have
is petty cash

I hope you turn to
see how far you've
come and all you're
worth,

before you turn to
ash

WEALTHY AT A COST

if anxiety was a
person,
he'd be a rich man

man, he loves to
screw you

rich, he owns real
estate in millions of
minds

sometimes, he rents
this space to tenants
including, but not
limited to self-hate,
self-doubt

and self-esteem
(who only ever
resides on the
lowest floor)

anxiety is a rich
man with a
dangerous degree of
power
but remember,

his fortune places
him in only the top
1 %

too tiny to be
worthy of your time

MARKET CAP ERROR

why do you use the
people
around you
to benchmark your
success?

as if they make up
the entire market,
it's outrageous

you will always
place yourself just
below average

no one will bet on
you if you only ever

classify yourself as
'undervalued'

SUPERMARKET
aisles

you make them

swerve in and out,

search back and
forth

uneasy to spot
swiftly.

like milk and bread

and eggs,

you are not a
commodity

limited edition,

reviews sublime,

quality unmatched,

6 am, they'll wait in
line

You are a luxury.

let them seek

and pursue you

the rise & fall

STORY TIME

unlike my bed
my mind was made
i couldn't picture a
better trade

it's true what they
say
it's give and it's
take
all of the strangers,
little mistakes

i left them behind
didn't know gentle,
didn't know kind

but you even make
sure
that i don't mind

and when they ask
me
if it was hard to
find,
i'll tell them in
chapters
starting with

"once upon a
time..."

ADVENTURE

we both knew a
person shouldn't be
the reason for our
happiness
but it was with each
other
where we felt the
happiest

we took a trip on a
Sunday,
back on Monday
we liked to move
like that
it was exciting and
fast

no phones, just a
map
cheap shoes, running
on naps
climbing trees and
racing back
to the beach and
down train tracks
we liked to live like
that

LESSONS FROM THE NEWS

In Sports:
do not get too high
on a winning streak.
do not get too low
on a losing streak

In Weather:
do not freak out
over todays'
temperature. It will
change tomorrow.

TABLE 88

they don't know you
have secret rooms

you only ever let
people into the
dining area

where you small talk
over dinner and

then when the meal
is over,

you are left alone,
sitting at your table

empty.

even after a full
meal,

you are empty and
you have no one to
blame but yourself

HIDE & SEEK

anger and hurt
like to play
hide and seek

and though it's been
days and weeks

hidden inside your
tainted heart

indeed,
they will show up
without a doubt

RECIPROCATION

you shouldn't go
through life with

a catcher's mitt on
both hands;

you need to be able
to throw something
back

COPACETIC

banter
and chemistry
and lines
dotted and crossed

and undeniable
passion
coupled with
disciplined
composure

an understanding
without the need for
words

how unfortunate it
is

good things all have
expiry dates

CHEERLEADER

took small
victories and
stacked them like
bricks,
made a pedestal
and I felt on top
of the world
because you put me
there

so, presumably, all
it took was removing
one block

like Jenga,

I

came

crashing

down

JANUARY FIRST

you always stole the
show,
didn't mind a crowd

the human version
of January 1st

people awaited your
arrival
and what a
celebratory welcome
causing quite a
ruckus,

but you are the start
of impractical
resolutions

the worst type of
unkept promises
the ones that spark
false hope,

fireworks and
emotional pollution

you ring in the new
year the same way

and expect a
different kind of
year

PLOT TWIST

beyond the deepest
valleys

and past the highest
peaks,

where the kings and
queens

crowned us rulers

cattle and castles

gardens and
waterfalls

even with everything
at my fingertips,
i still couldn't reach
you

i guess no one can
resist
a plot twist

how could i
have known your
velvet glove of
charm

hid an iron fist?

ZERO POINTS

all the letters on the
floor

I'm a light sleeper

but I didn't hear the
door

why was scrabble
your

favourite game

if you left without a
word

CLOCKWORK

I turned all the
lights on
when you left me
it wasn't even dark,
i was just lonely

think about
everything
you've shown me

guess you can have
it all but only
briefly

no red flags or
flashing signs

if the timing doesn't
align

it will never fall in
line

heartbreak week

GAME DAY

it wasn't game day
but you wore your
jersey
ready to play

should I mention,
serving a two game
suspension
in a different
dimension

much too high on
your winning streak
lack of defense made
your plan weak

penalties are not all
you killed

you,
on your powerplay
left me shorthanded

and it wasn't game
day
but you played me
anyway

PAY DAY

it wasn't payday
but I had to double
cheque
the note you wrote

listing everything I
owe
yet your balance
sheet didn't show

all that you had
borrowed

maybe you just
didn't know

the valuation of a
heart

so I had to pay,

and it was just a
Tuesday

TRASH DAY

you rolled me out
gently

it wasn't trash day
but

you put me out on
the curb anyway

GYM DAY

it wasn't gym day
but I lift you
anyway

the bruises you
leave
are sore in the
morning

lost you as quick as
my breath in cardio,
if only cellulite
could be gone as
fast as you go

sprinting at
breakneck speed
equipment - you
didn't need

but it wasn't gym
day
and maybe that's
why

we didn't work out

MAIL DAY

it wasn't mail day
but
you sealed me up,

walked to the
mailbox
dropped me in, with
a fragile label
not because I was
weak,

but because you had
already broken what
was to be
handled *with care*

anger, remorse, reflection

SORRY, WRONG

words like concrete
cemented in my head
i changed my number
but these memories
keep calling

SHAKESPERICAL

I wrote you dozens
of letters
on paper
and in my head

to ask you the
things people ask
about
in writing

if I could lessen, I
would,
the space between us
but I know
it is not with you,
my place

mostly I am just
wondering
if you've yet
laughed

the way I made you
laugh

CANVAS

you asked for a
circle;
I drew you the world

you wanted purple;
I gave you red
I gave you blue

that's when you
said,
I'm not keen on
listening
I just go ahead;
so maybe instead

we call it quits and
I nod my head

I put down the
crayons
in hindsight
knowing, colors
couldn't fill that
void of yours

you wanted purple
but I gave you blue;
I gave you red

could've mixed them
together
and created what
you said

REFUND PLEASE

I'd like to return your

store bought words

glow sticks

cheap tricks

can I get back my cash

for all your second hand trash?

FREE CAPTIVE

what an odd kind of
love,

neither was I held to
stay
nor
did I run away

HOW DID YOU KNOW?

I couldn't eat, I couldn't sleep

I saw a stranger that looked like him every day

WHAT WAS SHE LIKE?

like God used just
the right amount of
salt

not overpowering,

but

it's not the same
without her

NO ENDINGS

she never made it to
the end of a movie

always left the chat
on read

so many clothes on
her floor she needed
to fold
loves her coffee hot
but still lets it go
cold.

every series finale
she didn't watch yet

so many goodbyes,
none she'd regret

broken relation-
ships abandoned by
the shore
gets in bed at ten,
but doesn't sleep till
four

she should have told
me, perhaps she
didn't know then
that she only liked
the beginning of
things when

everything is new
and unknown; a
fresh, clean slate

I told her the ending
could be good
and if she wanted
to, I know she
probably could

but she preferred to
stay guarded,
keep it
light hearted

after all, she only
liked the way things
started

YEARS LATER

perhaps one day,
years later, we'll
meet again. In
another city, in
another time

and we will converse
with the kind of
terrible small talk
we once claimed to
hate

we'll dance around
the complicated
truth until our feet
give out

then we will sit
quietly, awaiting the
real confrontation

neither of us will
budge

for both our tidal
prides drowned this
friendship. It didn't
stand a chance
against the waves we
made

but

perhaps one day,
years later, we'll
get another chance

in a different city
in a different time

MISS ME ON
PURPOSE

I don't see your face
but I hear your name
still know that voice
I'll admit with
shame
avoid you all night
and you'll do the
same

late to the party,
I'm not surprised
walk in with that
sway I still despise

the people -
they should move
out of your way,
make room for that
ego as you do your
rounds of "Hey"

miss me on purpose
and that's more than
okay

interaction drains us
so we take our
breaks,
light it up for old
times' sake

now you're back at
the party but return
only partly
your eyes finally
meet me,
with the smile that
appears rarely

suddenly, I've
forgotten all their
names
I mean, I don't
really care

but I'm kind of glad
you came

ORDINARY

your eyes apologized
to me
and I forgave you
with a smile
yes, it's been a
while
yet
you've missed me,
I can tell
and I've always
wished you well

but I hope it drives
you crazy
because loving you

was lonely
dark, bright and sort
of hazy
maybe you deserve
ordinary

you didn't want to
lose me
but you did nothing
to keep me

FRAUD OF AN ARTIST

you drew
conclusions

you drew attention

you drew lines

that led me

 on
  and
     on

WELCOME TO
THERAPY

it's 3 am, I'm
waiting on you
I pack my bags, then
right on que

you waltz on in, the
session begins

untie the luggage on
top your chest,
before you speak I
hear the stress

still, I'm not very
good

at what I do
I never had the heart
to tell you

your lack of
character is the
reason why
you keep everything
in short supply
like emotions you
let run dry
and your hurt never
meets my eye

it travels straight
beyond my flesh

and makes me mad
that you can express

how you feel when
you're unimpressed
but not how your
heart needs some
rest

you recognize you're
full of doubt
but turn around and
talk about
work and news and
going out
you're tired and I'm
burning out

there is no fix for a
person that denies

being broken
what a waste of time
trying to refill an
ocean

the session ends
with the same
conclusion

and when you leave,
there is no clarity

you used me,

free therapy

ARCHITECT

I must blame my own
hands

for I built the shack

that housed your

insecurities

rent free

healing & empowerment

WHEN WINTER
ARRIVES

as i step outside,
the snow greets me
gently
and it feels like
i could just stand
here and watch the
grass turn white

these small
soft snowflakes
are warmer than
some people I've
met

WOKE

you were nothing
more than a pipe
dream

and

i am not sleeping
anymore

SILVER LINING

you become mad at
the world

the million and one
pieces that come
together to make the
world a whole

you hate all of it

and it kind of sucks
because

one day,

you wake up to
chirping birds

and the sun touching
you softly before it
hits the hardwood
floor

and you realize,

there is so much to
love

DIVINITY

we leave our houses
with full intents
on coming back

never stopping to
think
our return is
a blessing

PRAY

when I feel no peace
at my core
I only find solace on
the floor

It's true every time
I find that I'm

better in
remembrance of Him

GOODNESS

the first sip of
coffee in the
morning

climbing into bed
after a long day

and a hot shower

poutine with perfect
cheese to gravy
ratio

baby cheeks and
laughs

sleeping with no set
alarms

and waking up

with the gentle warm
sun in Spring

RESURGENCE

if you missed the
sunset,
go to sleep early
and catch the
sunrise

CHOOSE TO RISE

have you ever seen
the sun really
emerge?

not rise, but just
peak from the
distance

erupt from his
purplish orange
abyss
slowly, but fast
enough to miss if
you look away too
long

a fiery ball of red

furious, as if the
Lord pulled him out
of bed this morning,
telling him to go do
his job

a soft shine,
transforming into a
flashlight yellow

bright,
granting me
exclusive permission
to witness such a
sight

then, when he is
where he is
supposed to be,

he whispers to me

"I'm doing my job.
Now go do yours."

and when my day is
over, I see him
again

sinking, with the
same conviction in
which he rose,

but he's changed
now

more difficult for
my eyes to confront

maybe he had a
rough day too but
even still tomorrow,

he will rise

MONET

perchance, parts of
something must be
dysfunctional
to create an
exquisite bigger
picture

like the world
or our families

each has its issues
but together, as a
whole,
somehow, it can
still be *beautiful*

PERIPHERAL

some things are nice
to hear

but do not matter
anymore

GIFT RECIEPT

he wrapped up his
opinion
tightly with a bow,
hands it to me
swiftly

*"It's my opinion,
you can have it."*
as-a-matter-of-fact
sort of way

"That's okay," I say,

*"I already have my
own."*

ELASTIC

some men see a
strong women

as an invitation, or
a challenge

to see how quickly
they can break her

but are left
frustrated

when they are faced
with rubber and not
glass

KINDNESS

an ounce
of kindness
comes back
tenfold

ACCEPTANCE

cultivate
acceptance,
not confidence

accept that you can
feel ugly some days
accept that you
don't know the
answer
accept that you are
flawed
accept that you have
lots to offer
accept that you are
lovely and loved

accept the apology
you owe yourself

confidence comes
through acceptance

when you accept all
that is and all that
can be,

confidence will
emerge

GIVING

giving has the power
to fill my hollows
so I will not stop
until every crevice
in me is
utterly overflowing
with satisfaction

MEMENTO MORI

in the times of the
ancient romans,
there was a Latin
phrase they used
often, "memento
mori", meaning
remember death

back then, death was
seen as a motivator
to do good, to live a
meaningful life

remembering death
is a reminder to live

after all, life is a
series of
extraordinary
experiences

they all end
but then,

so do we

THE END

these days will
disappear,
turn into years that
you will miss
like others before it
that felt just like
this

and you will be left
wondering,
perhaps even
wishing,

you could run back
as fast as you ran
away

ON HAPPINESS

I learned

the only way to be
happy

is to want

what you already
have

SELF CHECK:

you have enough to
fill your stomach
but *what feeds your
soul?*

THANK YOU,
SINCERELY...
you made it to the end!
(special thanks to romiasa)

I wrote poems as an
creative outlet but I
wasn't aware it would
turn into a project that
would challenge and
uplift me the way that
it has.

Some of these poems
were written five or
six years ago. I was a
different person with a
totally different
perspective on life. I
almost didn't publish
some of my earlier

pieces because I didn't agree with what I had written or thought I sounded immature but it was, in a way, amazing to see how I had developed as a writer and as a person.

I've always loved to write but sometimes I would just stop. for weeks or even months. I found that writing on my own terms, without holding myself to any standard allowed my words to flow more naturally. I didn't think I could be inspired by my own

writing but I go back
and read and think
'damn, I wrote that.
That's pretty cool.'

Appreciate yourself.
reflect on how far
you've come.
celebrate. create
things that make you
happy.

Thank you for reading
and supporting

all my love,

bea.
x